BY THE SAME AUTHOR

CLABBER STREET BLUES

CLABBER STREET BLUES

JOSEPH ALLEN

Greenwich Exchange
London

Acknowledgements

Abridged, Acumen, Agenda, Ambit, Cyphers, FourXFour, The Shop, South Carolina Review, Stand, The Stony Thursday Book and *The Ulster Folk.*

Greenwich Exchange, London

First published in Great Britain in 2016
All rights reserved

Printed and bound by imprintdigital.net
Cover design by December Publications
Tel: 07951511275

Greenwich Exchange Website: www.greenex.co.uk

Cataloguing in Publication Data is available from the British Library

Cover art: Thelonius Monk
© Mary Evans Picture Library/Everett Collection

ISBN: 978-1-910996-07-2

CONTENTS

BACK ROADS

Sit me in front of the television,
a heel of White Chief
toasted and buttered.

Lead me through the woods
with Ma and Pa Pogle
or over the hills
opposite the Wooden Tops' farm,
tramp upon heavy tramp
along the country roads.

Eighty years tomorrow
my mother died,
I will follow her soon,
Autumn lowers its melancholy head
among the hedgerows and fields,
a contented weariness
cradles my head.

RUE 29 JUILLET

Tourists crowd the Tuileries,
the reflected sun
from white sand round the Plane trees
blinds my eyes,
children bathe in the fountains
as their parents bask in the heat.

Paris lounges in the sun,
the Luxembourg Gardens
extend a welcome
to my soul
and asks, why, what are you here for?

A quiet afternoon
on a café terrace
is disrupted by an alcoholic,
she offers me bread and cheese
from her handbag,
tries to kiss me
like a lover,
the city has lost its charms –
I'm looking for another metropolis.

SILVER SPOON

The metal spoon
forces its way
between clenched teeth.

The smell and taste
of rotten potato
causes me to retch,
vomit on to the plate,
once again I feel it in my mouth.

A battle of strength,
he thinks hunger will make me eat,
I starve against his will.

I press the food
between his lips
accept his refusal.

LESSONS

Escaping from class,
sitting in the reference library,
hiding among the shelves,
the unemployed and the lost.

Copying Perseus, arm outstretched,
the snake-haired head
held tightly in his fist.

My father forces me,
to conquer his fears,
I triumph
in each failure tried anew.

SEASONS

Morning passes slowly,
the cold room unaffected
by the small heater,
a pile driver echoes
across the dreary streets,
its rhythmic thud
mirroring my mood.

I close my eyes,
feel the heat on the Via Santa Giustina,
pass deformed, silent beggars,
a quartet plays Vivaldi
outside the San Michele,
approaching I realise
all four are blind,
oblivious to the passing tourists,
flash bulbs, dropped coins.

MY UNCLE'S HOUSE

I search for my uncle's house,
look among the extensions and renovations,
the long gone hedgerows
blocking my view of the railway track.

Listen for those Friday afternoons,
the joy of newly opened pay packets,
the weight of another week's toil
washed away at a kitchen sink.

My uncle had a girlfriend,
vindictive in her love,
tried to win me over
in her childish ways.

I pass her each morning,
the only two about at that hour,
watch her searching through the rubbish bins,
unable to share our pain.

BLUE SKIES

A perfect afternoon,
the uninterrupted blue sky,
trees gently swaying in the breeze.

To die now,
or end it oneself
would be satisfaction,
but only if you could be assured
of a similar afternoon
to reflect on one's passing.

The dandelions more vivid
than the primrose yellow
in the watercolour box
bought with saved pocket money
on a Sunday evening
in McGroggans.

These thoughts are lost
on this country road,
the night deadening their echoes.

MARBLE

Because I knew her so,
this lifeless body is foreign.

These hands never soothed me
with their softness.

These breasts never comforted me
with their warmth.

I kiss the cold brow,
the closed eyes,
the lips silenced forever.

Her memory
alive within me.

MORNING

My eyes open,
become accustomed to the dim light
of the curtained room.

I make out the forms of sleepers
filling the chairs and floor,
inhale the stale air
from last night's cigarettes.

Dressing I prepare breakfast,
'The Chorus of the Hebrew Slaves'
plays on the stereo,
wakening the others.

We finish the leftover beers,
open a bottle of brandy,
I feel the alcohol take effect,
wonder how much longer
I can live like this.

FAREWELL

As we reach the village
I notice little change
from the time I passed through
to work at the quarry,
the flags still fly from lampposts,
marking out territories.

This chapel the same
from when I attended a brother's wedding,
the two families separated
by more than an aisle.

As the body is carried in
I recognise the 'Ashokan Farewell',
feel guilty at criticising the musicians,
watch you shoulder a father's weight.

Only a fortnight before
I sat by my mother's bed,
watched the rise and fall of her breast
each time more laboured,
a voice repeating,
that's it, that's her now.

METRONOME

With each death
we close on mortality,
stand in the tradition
of our past.

Those silent Sundays
shed with the years,
have dropped their drawn afternoons
like amber leaves.

Each echoing image
of a passing life
remains on our skin
as personal stigmata.

Scars form memories,
a rosary of days,
the counting of time.

THE DAWN

I lie watching
the slow drip to my arm,
drowse off, awaken,
see nurses pass in the corridor,
catch their small talk.

I am in isolation,
the hours pass slowly
and the pain gone
I just want to leave,
hate the disruption to my night.

It is early morning,
I stand in the rain
hoping each coming headlight
is my taxi,
two young girls smoke beside me,
wet make-up streaking their faces,
the sky pales with the dawn.

SPACE

My first cries
acclaimed the space age,
gulping lungfuls of cold air
in a brittle January morning.

And I think Yuri
must have felt the same
aboard Chertok's Vostok 1,
breaking through to an unknown world.

My mother and I,
on a screened-off bed,
survivors both
in the zero hour.

Boris and my mother
dying months apart,
fifty years on
from that winter of discovery.

CLASS

Neglected, undeserving of attention,
sitting in the back rows,
ignored, unless causing a disturbance.

Our appearance
at the front of the class
when we were called last
for free school meal tickets.

We sat our eleven plus unprepared
and still held our own,
upsetting expectations.

Now, with hindsight,
I realise the segregation,
how our addresses
mapped out our future.

CHINESE HAT

When I listen to 'Ruby, My Dear'
or 'Crepuscule with Nellie'
and Monk hits
that unexpected note,
I understand his genius.

He rises, dances,
plays the intro from 'Round Midnight',
his dissonance
reflecting my uncertainty.

Monk does not fit in,
he stands alone,
aloof from life,
inspiring me to rebel,
have faith in my oneness.

I sing the song,
the music comes from within,
the instrument is my voice,
it tells a truth without words.

FISH TANK

The fish tank spins before my eyes,
each Saturday hour
passing like eternity,
I have learned the patience
of a prisoner,
how to ignore hands of the clock.

The family's weight
upon my shoulders,
I pass the graveyard,
Howie's Pink
tight in my hand,
a father's drunken breath on my face.

I see that childish self,
head swathed in bed clothes,
hiding from his fears,
imagined and real,
ignorant of the future.

MIRROR

Age looks in the mirror,
waiting its cue,
drifting like clouds over Park Head,
trains passing beyond the convent walls.

Can that be me,
walking the back road home,
pass the overgrown gardens,
the billy goats with slatted eyes.

I feel older than the teachers,
whose knowledge stops at school,
not theirs, the reality of home,
the betrayal of childhood.

I hate their nature tables,
the Halloween masks, nativity plays,
their attempts to have me participate,
I keep myself apart, secure.

FLAX MILL, DERRYLANE

Hermann is host,
passing round broth, wheaten, potato salad,
refilling glasses.

All day, Marion and Hermann
have been welcoming visitors –
for nineteen years
they have been running
their open days.

With the artists' dinner complete
we musicians take to the stage,
music knows no borders,
different traditions blend,
complement each other.

The night is country black,
no electric lights obscure the stars,
music and voices travel
far in the sharp air.

Tomorrow, Hermann
will be waist deep in the dam,
soaking the flax
legs numb in the cold water,
the hum of the generator
from the mill.

Winter born.
This is how days turn,
not suddenly, unaware
but in creeping routine,
the drawing of blinds
at evening's close.

Hours hang like cobwebs
on frosted hedges,
pass like wind in the trees.

We are winter born,
children of the hard ground,
inured to the cold of rooms,
the bite of hunger.

Our youth is old,
blown across abandoned schoolyards,
squandered on factory floors,
haunting remembered days.

PÈRE LACHAISE

To come upon someone's grief,
that private communion,
on a sunny morning
absentmindedly reading the inscriptions
like some browser in a second-hand bookshop.

Watching the wiping of tears,
the ritual arranging of flowers,
lips moving in prayer,
a hand brushing hair from the forehead.

Stand still, do not disturb this moment,
listen to the noises beyond the wall,
feel the heat from the ground,
her movements calm as the sky.

VALUES

The bridge connects the town,
behind the estate, a wooded path,
private houses, watch-tower and lawns.

Signing on, Monday morning,
facing the cold,
to the dole office,
civil servants pissed off with another week,
pushing their resentments on to us –

who are not them,
not tied to a mortgage,
a pension, dwindling with the years,
trying to write my way out.

I'd like to be registered in no file,
slipping through the fingers,
not a statistic.

My parents' child,
raised to their values,
pushed into a world
they'll never know.

THE KING OF ITALY'S LIBRARY

I feel alone in this blue room
the empty streets below
years have passed unnoticed
ignored by the young –
I defy the hours
sleep may separate my body and soul
as I awake in this foreign city
so do not remind me
of how we touched
because I reject the knowledge of love.

LIMBO

My mother sang,
to the background
of Sunday morning television,
her song rising from the kitchen.

'The Banks of the Foyle'
ringing with the steel comb
through my medicated head,
nits washed down the kitchen sink.

These mornings never pass,
I lie in limbo,
listen to my sister's albums,
awakening a love of music.

Still I hear my mother's song
caressing me from within,
the tune's refrain forever sounds
in a melody I sing again.

LITTLE ASHES

Lorca, I too suffer,
a country torn in half.

I feel the need to escape,
to leave.

Eli, call me one more time,
with my father's voice I answer.

I am Aaron,
my faith falters but is strong.

Bury me in little ashes,
there is more than one way
to kill a poet.

APPRENTICESHIP

Hips, Haws and Fuchsias
colour Patton's depot.

Childish disputes are settled
among the Laurel bushes.

Saint Louis dispatches its convent girls
onto Mount Street
my sexual awakening begins.

The youth who apprenticed his years,
raised on hard bread and fists,
growing into himself.

And parents, laid together in the grave,
who never knew.

MY SISTER'S COUSIN

I want to tear your ballerina dresses,
your George Best posters,
lay waste your privileged childhood.

My first taste of coffee,
tomato soup, hot chocolate,
came from your father's mobile shop.

My sister, a travelling companion,
to your boredom,
a plain child, to contrast your beauty.

A mother's visits timed
to avoid embarrassing your in-laws.

A silence against the roar
of the tide pounding on the shore.

FORGOTTEN DAYS

Down the weary avenue
run the forgotten days,
and each spring blossom
records the season's death.

The school bell sounds
across the dam,
and late I know
the park's arrested time
delays my steps.

The summer sun
arises from the pines,
voices rise and fall
sleepy with the day.

I wonder where the falling voices rest,
the calling of parents
ignored and lost
and soon the shadows lose their shapes
and I am thrust
into a morning's whitened gaze.

PASSPORT

I change addresses with abandon
like Lacey's trek through South America,
his endless boys a search back to himself.

An afternoon in Salat
I picked at chicken,
watched the tourists crisscross the square,
a girl with Mexican eyes
passes to and fro.

American students cram the train
I listen to their endless talk,
oblivious to the passing countryside
they talk of careers, families, college.

I feel my isolation,
an outsider to their youth,
a world passed beyond me
a form outside their sight.

These people have no need
their sorrows to seek,
they await their fate patiently
like Job's eternal why.

THE UNHEARD WORD

So we sang
and our song became the past,
voices rose from impoverished streets
and rattled against the windows of the schools.

We were the unheard word,
dragged from schoolyard to factory,
screaming out from the class.

My father blamed his children
for the years,
the hours of loneliness,
shared with a wife he couldn't love.

Both gone, I no longer seek explanations,
having reached their age,
full of questions,
looking for closure.

GENERATIONS

Through childhood, I became a man,
warped by experience
but straight in other ways.

My father might have loved me,
an affection for his issue,
but somewhere, we came to hate.

My mother tore her heart,
a buffer between us,
I cannot hate her for her pain.

Now they are gone,
I, their sole connection with this earth,
feel no anger at their mistakes.

I have no children,
no desire to replicate myself,
I near death and relaxation.

I have no explanation for the next generation,
why they must suffer
years of uncertainty.

We are born, we die,
such is life,
programmed onto our end.

All we leave behind
are work, art, thoughts,
cast them aside,
they cost us nothing
but the soul.

BURDENS

A man feels the burden of his years,
learns to accept his failings,
passes his knowledge on.

Each life adds to the next,
our children reject us
as theirs reject them.

We are stoical,
learn the certainty of death.

I do not dispute this,
wonder, why a God
feels this must be.

RAIDER'S MOON

We wake on the road to Lyon,
wet with dew,
looking for a meal,
and I think of Curls Avenue,
searching for balsa,
weary with heat
and ready for home.

I want to take you
over the Alleghenys,
carve out a life,
fight with the scalping parties
by the light of a raider's moon.

This routine wears on me,
days unfold on days,
we fight each other's boredom,
unravel habit's threads,
looking for something we fear to find.

RECALL THE HOURS

And if I leave
remember me occasionally,
recall the hours,
the hedgerow smells
and the fields stretching out of sight.

We will not pass again,
similar lives will walk these roads,
enjoy the shade,
spend an afternoon.

The summer will end,
Autumn unfurls its colours
and days will pass before our eyes.

Days roll out their hours,
lives, their days,
the uncertainty of time before us.

CHAINS

Like an aunt
who knew life's woes
I fought against each chain.

Childhood's hours,
longer than the days
would hang upon my head.

His footsteps
on the garden path
sounded the close of day.

A bedroom's cold
takes time to pass,
fading into sleep.

And I have come
into this world,
free from blood and bone.

LA DONCELLA

I near my end,
alcohol numbs my days,
the bitter taste of cocoa leaves,
I look for my family
knowing they are gone.

I see people on this mountain,
I see no one on this mountain,
we talk, pass the time,
I watch them come and go,
but I must stay.

Is that the sun,
a new one
or the same that rose this morning,
I lose count
of each passing day.

I must have slept,
I awake, lost, confused,
where is my family,
I lost them somewhere.

Who left these bottles,
I drink and drink,
not knowing why
but knowing I must keep on.

The eagle is above,
circling the sky,
I do not need to watch,
it will always be there.

I can no longer lift my head,
the sky must pass
without my gaze,
my body flies,
I watch it from afar,
alone I spend my days.

I am abandoned,
I know my death is near,
who will mourn my passing,
no one to watch my end.

My body will rest here forever,
undisturbed by man,
no one will know my lonely grave.

DON'T SAY FRISCO

Breakfast is served by teams,
vying against each other,
their attention lasting long enough
to serve and move you out.

The Seven To Eleven
makes mostly on passing trade,
especially, after hours,
pizza and Coor's Lite.

Standing in line,
voices spin around your head,
'No, no, no mama,
Pepperoni',
I stand with my pound cake and beer.

Just off the Golden Gate
we eat chilli dogs and fries,
day trippers to Sausalito ask directions,
mistake us for locals.

Down on Columbus
the dancing waiter serves beer,
says he likes my Hot Rats T-shirt,
curls the ends of his moustache
and side steps back to the bar.

BASEBALL

Near the warming hut
I missed an easy catch,
misjudging the bounce
the ball dropping through
the clear air.

And I felt like Jackson,
balancing bottles of beer
on a bicycle frame,
or Basquiat
in his cardboard bed.

The senses dull
at times like these,
embarrassed at our awkwardness,
our heavy-handed existence.

The volunteers are out in force
repairing the pathways,
dogs chase Frisbees,
children try to manage
the mechanics of bike riding.

The afternoons pass regardless,
families pack up picnics,
street lamps flicker,
the city glows.

ISLANDS

Free to stretch without restriction,
no televised racing
droning in my ears.

To search for breadfruit
in far off seas
and follow Mr Christian
to his fate.

To live off the bounty
of these islands,
with only the ticking clock
marking my passing freedom.

The fading light
sees off the afternoon's hours,
my father is home from work,
Bligh is cast adrift
and with him my mutiny
is washed away.

JUDITH

I think of you on the line,
trying to match the skill,
the speed of the local women,
the nauseating smell of fish,
unable to understand the conversation.

And what did they make of you,
the minister's wife,
newly arrived on the islands,
working with them each day,
unlike the others they had known?

You said the Faroese
were slow to accept,
wary of a stranger's ways,
but patience and God would see you through
the life you had left behind.

And in the dark and stormy nights,
you became used to another's body,
the sounds crashing around you, around the house,
these islands you would come to know as home,
an isolation, a question mark of the past.

VENTRILOQUIST

Leaving the town behind,
we'd pause on the brow of the hill,
looking back,
like Fante stepping through
a bedroom window
from the street below.

How the fishery stifled him,
the Mexican workers
unwilling to accept his presence.

Or Bukowski on the sorting line,
dreading every routine test,
living for the pen, six-pack and quart,
and Voss forever on the production line.

Myself on a ten-hour shift,
six days a week,
trying to make poems
out of stolen moments.

A factory in a town,
like all the rest.

BABY, PLEASE DON'T GO

Weekend trips to Belfast,
Winnie's painting-by-numbers,
Maud and Hannah's ham and tea.

Chips and shakes
in The Milky Way
before the evening train.

Watching Them in Paris,
1965,
Morrison sang like he meant it
and I was four years old.

The shutters came down
on the second-hand bookshops
as we left Smithfield far behind,
rocking to sleep on the return,
the town unfamiliar in the dark,
'Baby, Please Don't Go'
tucked under my arm.

ENTERPRISE

Such a peaceful afternoon,
backs against the wall
feet stretched towards the railway,
drinking Concorde.

An unruly crew
on the minimum wage,
afraid of nothing.

But we have the sun
and each other,
a disregard of everything.

We walk the line into town,
cash our money,
kings for the weekend,
until Monday.

A LETTER TO HANK

Where was Hank back then
when I needed him most,
five years old, abandoned in the schoolyard,
lost among my classmates,
looking for a helping hand.

No oranges ripening in the Californian sun,
a Sunday raid upon the orchards,
I felt his father's belt upon my back
so many times before.

His no-neck bride
smiles from a wedding shot,
like my family photos
forgotten in some plastic bag.

Yet poems force through
our broken lives,
connected with each other,
and fathers fall.

AMONG THE TREES

Smoking on the Bois de Boulogne
people walk dogs, read papers,
picnic, meet lovers.

The lights fade, cars park,
night descends upon the tree-lined paths.

From my seat I watch a couple
leave the road,
disappear among the trees,
argue about the price.

OPEN EARTH

Each funeral brings us closer
to the grave,
gazing on the open earth.

My mother feared her death
much more than rent arrears or tick,
each Sunday evening
she passed her grocery list to me.

I watched her relenting every chore,
each one a part of her,
an acceptance of passing strength.

Her weight upon my shoulder
is somehow comforting,
a passing of generations,
the continuance of days
beyond ourselves.

PLANTERS

We lost ourselves on country roads,
hours passed unnoticed,
time became suspended.

The Greek helmets
arranged in rows
before the water treatment plant.

Our hand claps raising the rooks
behind Crebilly graveyard,
sneaking a look
inside the chapel,
a world we would never know.

A car horn blasted in passing,
a tricolour waved in the wind
unaware of our indifference.

Cider bottles flung from the bridge,
we make our way home,
singing the Blues as we pass
between the blossoming hawthorns.

LISTENING TO WOLVES

I walked the smoothing iron
with Boris Karloff,
listened to the wolves
howling by the Devil's Cup
and wondered at women
giving birth in the Cottage
across the lake.

Miss Jessel watches
my infant self,
throwing crusts upon the water,
attracting the birds of terror
around my shoes.

My aunt's leathered feet
afraid of the wet leaves,
the reek of sodden laundry
forever in the house.

An uncle waiting twenty years
for my understanding,
the mother, son,
I thought I knew
becoming brother and sister.

FREAKS

And so we sat,
three twelve-year-olds
drinking frothy coffee.

Listening to bands,
letting our hair grow wild.

I dropped out
but kept in touch,
you worked in a bookshop,
ordered me *À la Recherchè du Temps Perdu*
and *The Man Without Qualities*,
I wondered if you recognised us.

And the other one
I met in the tropics
of the Botanic hothouse,
writing songs, dreaming.

As I release each poem
into the world,
like our lives.

THE BLUES

Each Sunday afternoon
I walked the deserted streets,
my feet in the Mississippi Delta,
Jackson's Corner
sounding like somewhere
Furry could be from.

I was part of a secret,
of Champion Jack, Otis,
Chicken Shack, Blue Horizon.

How did an East End Jew
connect with these songs?

Each generation sings the blues,
changes are made
yet remain unchanged.

STEPS

The places walked
will outlive our steps,
like the lights of Avignon
seen from a passing bus shine on.

The light reflected
from shattering glass,
time slowed to fill a room.

The shining metal of police
upon the stairs
and the cooling air
of night upon our skin.

The sound of feet
along the house backs
breaking the darkness.

ENDLESS DAYS

One of those afternoons
deadened, as the sun refused to rise.

The high lonesome sound
from the wireless
and the melancholy
of childhood's endless days.

My senses dulled
Like a bullet to the head,
Lorca's lost days
on a hillside,
the shade of trees.

The living's in the writing,
we live each word,
caress every perfect phrase.

CLABBER STREET

The sun doesn't shine on Clabber Street,
the winos drink Special Brew, Silver Crown
as the shoppers rush to their parked cars.

The drunken tinker
lifts her skirt
and laughs at the people passing.

In your flat
the empty stout bottles
are kept out of view
with the Good News chocolates
you received on your son's death.

And the World War veteran,
throwing a grocery list and money
to the youths below,
means nothing to you.

The chapel bells
interrupt your sleep
awaken your guilt and thirst.

And the drunk lover
taking back his money
from your pocket,
unaware of your indifference.

SOUR HILL

Each day, the music drew me,
but the cottage door
held me from my fate.

The sound of fiddle and mandolin
lured me from my home.

Until Sam took me in,
endured my endless questions,
my childish attempts at music.

The di'el among the tailors
enticed me with its trill.

I ached to sound its notes,
just once, to play the 'Ashokan Farewell',
'Fire Upon the Mountain', 'Soldier's Joy'.

The connection of history,
passed through each tune,
an acceptance of the past.

* di'el: Local pronunciation for 'devil'

THE GLOBE

I watched the neighbours
cross the green,
listened to Rory,
drew the smoke in deep,
an afternoon of lessons in my head.

Spent a lunch hour as a sentinel,
looking for someone
to place my father's bet.

A brother, escaped from the factory,
expects his lunch,
gives me a cigarette,
waits for his lift.

Friday art classes
spent in The Globe,
a truant teacher
passing small talk at the bar.

PERFORMANCE

I watch the neighbours,
their uneventful days pass,
lives spent in trivia.

And I am no better,
years have passed,
I plan my future
and ignore the present.

Who hears my song
played each night
to a weary audience
seeking oblivion?

I take from them
what they cannot give,
a truth I keep untold
and lives must spend
each troubled day
until the end unfolds.

THE POWER OF WORDS

The New English Bible
was a disappointment,
Ezekiel and Eli never spoke these words.

Gone, the poetry of the King James,
the mystery of another age.

The Song of Solomon,
sang to me from the page,
burning my childish tongue.

My grandfather's voice shone
like the peal of bells
as he read to me.

The power of words
filling my senses with an understanding
that would last for years.

GHOSTS

Are the ghosts of my ghosts
whispering along Church Lane,
heard through Sidney Street
in the fading light?

On a wet afternoon
I watched my mother pass
and all around the everyday went on.

Another self calls out
from across the dam
familiar and unsettling.

A great silence enveloped me,
a dream of time
confusing my senses.

PAPIER MÂCHÉ

Our parents accepted them,
match-box holders, beaten ashtrays
flying ducks, swimming fish
churned out by the thousands,
the product of each generation.

Where have they gone,
filling a millennium of landfill sites
like the cards for Mother's Day,
Father's Day, Easter, Christmas,
toiled over by each tortured brow?

They have disappeared
like their recipients,
and we in turn accept our due.

What is meant by these misshapen lumps of clay,
paper plate Halloween masks?

And what of those
who smash the papier mâché heads,
squash the egg-carton creations
of childish dreams?

SPRING

My sister has taken
her Carpenters and Bread albums,
the Friday afternoon treats,
the Gallagher cheques.

We were never close,
or so I thought
but now I feel her hand upon me.

I was always the one
who turned up on her doorstep,
all-night sessions with my guitar.

Now, I miss her,
a long gone spring.

BAPTISMAL

The days passed
following each other
with the same monotony
of cars coming and going
in the dull, heavy heat of the afternoon.

I can still see my uncle
forever pushing his world war bike
past the park gates,
whistling songs from the hit parade,
dreaming of girls and Saturday nights.

I have reached the age he was then
but still feel my boyhood
rushing by the hoardings,
the weight of generations
on my childish frame.

Once I was left behind
during a fire drill,
wandering the empty corridors
with the alarms echoing my steps,
and turning each corner
I eagerly expected an inferno.

With an aunt I fed stale bread
to the ducks in the dam,
felt her hand upon my back,
the sudden wetness on my face.

With wonder I listened
as my mother was told
how I fell into the water,
too engrossed with the ducks
to mind my step.

And I still love my crazy aunt,
stealing flowers from the convent,
saying Hail Marys on a found rosary,
mixing religions to fill her needs
and seeing each crucifixion as her own.

DOUBTING THOMAS

Did Thomas have his doubts
confirmed by a mission
he wanted to refuse?

Amongst Buddhists, Jains, Hindus,
did he look for a Christ to cling to?

Among his fellow Apostles
did he feel his uselessness,
the hopelessness of his faith?

And I too doubted,
wondered at a religion
that ignored me in poverty,
balked at washing my unclean feet.

I longed for Old Testament prophets,
appearing as fiery tongues,
chastising with scorpions,
taking an eye for an eye.

How I detested those Sunday preachers,
their faith bound to a weekly routine,
unwilling to accept my private devotion.

NIGHT IN TUNISIA

I can picture myself
in the Forties,
brilliantined hair,
a cigarette case of Gallagher Greens.

Listening to Miles,
feeling superior to
the pop loving teens.

I should have been a man in '61,
living in the post-war boom
an abundance of factory girls on my arm.

In '79 I made my break,
bumming around France
until the Consulate paid my fare home.

A father envious of my mistakes
drove me from the family home,
six months too late to make a point.

Hard times around Lyons
had hardened me
to a vagrant's life.

I could feel his shame
as he drove by,
my indifference camped on a street corner,
oblivious to him.

Place me in Minton's,
listening to Bird, Dizzy and Monk
cutting the changes,
I belong here,
In the cigarette smoke around the horns.

BLACK DOGS

Churchill walks our black dogs
on the beach,
his conversation wandering with his thoughts.

And what am I doing here,
matching my stride
to a lost generation.

My school books are dog eared and forgotten,
before the age of recycling.

I lose myself in Stalingrad,
among the British Expeditionary Force,
Spion Kop, Rorke's Drift, the Crimea.

I am a collector of medals,
a magpie assembling
my glittering gallery.

I lay my head upon the block
of future generations,
the unforgiving judgement of youth.

TAR BABIES

Each Sunday morning was a chaos of activity,
tripping over one another in a house too small.

The bedlam of breakfast,
washing of school uniforms,
housework, homework, a father's hangover,
I found a space to read.

Br'er Rabbit was my hero,
escaping every ingenious trap,
my favourite was the Tar Baby,
unable to let go.

And as I grew older we had our own tar babies,
a warning to the local girls.

I wondered how they met the morning,
the shame of exposure,
thrown into the briars.

NEW & RECENT POETRY
FROM GREENWICH EXCHANGE

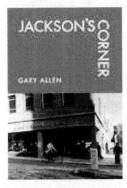

JACKSON'S CORNER
Gary Allen
£11.99 (pbk) ♦ 94pp ♦ 2016
978-1-910996-03-4

Poetic fashions come and go but true artistic vision remains. Standing outside the cosy circles of influence and scorning the easy immediacies of the glossy supplements, Gary Allen has honed his craft to produce a body of work which will undoubtedly endure.

Jackson's Corner sees Allen returning to his chosen ground of provincial Northern Ireland, in his case the County Antrim town of Ballymena. Named after a town landmark where people met, shopped, fell in and out of love, this collection sees Allen turn his attention to lives lived beyond the traditional gazes of art; and to lives often unrecorded, unconsidered, and, largely, unmourned.

He brings to his task not just poetic skill but a painful honesty. The poems of *Jackson's Corner* are not sentimental celebrations of 'little' people. Rather Allen's poems deal with them in all their complexity, in all their meanness and in all their grandeur.

These are compelling and harrowing poems.

MATELOT
Michael Cullup
£11.99 (pbk) ♦ 132pp ♦ 2016
978-1-906075-95-8

Often forgotten in the popular imagination, the National Serviceman still has his tale to tell.

Michael Cullup's long poem *Matelot* vividly recaptures the experiences of those who saw service aboard ship in the Royal Navy. Centring on the experiences of an Engineer Mechanic, *Matelot* describes life as it was then – the coarse language, the fights, the drunkenness, and, above all, the sterling comradeship.

It is, now, a time long gone, never to return. *Matelot* gives the reader some idea of what it was like to be part of it all – in its miseries, in its excitements and pleasures.

And in all its anarchic glory, too.

a rainbow of only one hue

simon david

£11.95 (pbk) ♦ 96pp ♦ 2016
978-1-910996-99-7

The full spectrum of writing within *a rainbow of only one hue* is a widening range of poems poignantly pigmented by the colourful. Uniquely used language stretches words across themes predominantly relationship based. The arch of these relationships disperses varying measures of light and dark, brightly shading a vividly vibrant view imaginatively spectacular in style. A radiant realism resplendently reveals the end of the rainbow to be an ink pot of passion infused in the hue of blue.

A blue rich in rhythmic rhymes that chimes over today's times with words tinted in textures diversely dense in every sense.

THE MEMORY TREE

Sean Haldane

£9.99 (pbk) ♦ 90pp ♦ 2015
978-1-906075-94-1

The Memory Tree: Poems 2009-2015 is Sean Haldane's first collection since the publication of his collected poems, *Always Two* (2009). As in all his work, the poems of *The Memory Tree* display an impressive intellectual and aesthetic clarity, married to a refreshing candour about the joys and pains of love and desire. Haldane brings to his work an authoritative, confident voice but one capable of a reflective questioning, a playful sense of irony and an unashamed belief in the redemptive power of lyric poetry as he explores the theme and counter-theme of the past and present.

ENDGAME

POEMS: NEW & USED

Gordon Jarvie

£11.99 (pbk) ◆ 80pp ◆ 2016
978-1-910996-98-0

Endgame sees the poet Gordon Jarvie continuing the biographical approach of his major selected poems, *A Man Passing Through: Memoir with Poems* (Greenwich Exchange, 2014).

Here are ruminations on mortality and advancing age, Scottish letters, landscape and local life, and time spent in Africa. A determination to live a life laced with laughter shines through. Jarvie's poems achieve sharp focus and emotional depths: this body of work which will endure.

A MAN PASSING THROUGH

MEMOIR WITH POEMS SELECTED & NEW

Gordon Jarvie

£16.99 (pbk) ◆ 252pp ◆ 2014
978-1-906075-89-7

A Man Passing Through is writer and editor Gordon Jarvie's autobiography in poetry.

Loosely chronological, this Selected Poems (comprising about half the poems of a consistently productive career) is a wry, witty and insightful collection, gathering together the various strands making up an ordinary life – family, early years, student days, the publishing trade, holidays in Brittany, climbing in the Scottish mountains, retirement in Fife, birdwatching, getting older, and many others.

Taken together *A Man Passing Through* stands as a remarkable portrait of a life lived in, and through, letters.

PORTABLE PROPERTY
John Lucas

£9.99 (pbk) ♦ 82pp ♦ 2015
978-1-910996-00-3

The poems of John Lucas's latest collection, *Portable Property*, crackle with wit and insight, creating and recreating worlds at once familiar and original. Whether writing in a shorter lyric form, prose poems or long narrative pieces like 'Don Johnson, Restaurateur', Lucas brings to his work an acute observational skill allied to a compassion for all-too-human weaknesses.

With an ear for the colloquial, Lucas draws from the telling minutiae of the everyday, tackling head on the great themes and, in the process, producing poetry recognisably of the English lyric tradition: unfussily modest, comprehensible and engaging the reader in a real place and time.

Portable Property shows Lucas to be a true craftsman.

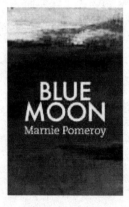

BLUE MOON
Marnie Pomeroy

£9.99 (pbk) ♦ 76pp ♦ 2015
978-1-910996-02-7

This collection begins with dawn that turns into a fox and ends beyond black space with a monocle moon on its eye. In between, common characters are brought to life: the sun and his ferocious smile; a jealous telephone pole; a lovelorn chimney; creaturely water in many habitats; Night, berserk, performing his Wind Concerto; and various trees, persons, and moons – a blue moon being the rare, second full moon to occur within a month.

Blue Moon showcases Marnie Pomeroy's unique and creative voice.

COME CLOSE AND LISTEN
Jim C. Wilson
£9.99 (pbk) ◆ 88pp ◆ 2014
978-1-906075-85-9

In a writing career spanning three decades Jim C. Wilson has mapped out his own territory in Scottish letters with his work drawing praise for its combination of astute vision and skilled lyric craftsmanship.

Whether writing about nature, landscape, memory and mortality, the uncertainties and joys of love, Wilson in *Come Close and Listen* brings to his subjects an unpretentious but telling poetic authority.

To find out more about these and other titles visit
www.greenex.co.uk

GREENWICH EXCHANGE SELECTED POETRY LIST

Gary ALLEN
Jackson's Corner
£11.99 (pbk) ♦ 94pp ♦ 2016
978-1-910996-03-4

Charles BAUDELAIRE
Les Fleurs du Mal (edited F.W. Leakey)
£9.95 (pbk) ♦ 160pp ♦ 1997
978-1-871551-10-5

Maggie BUTT
Lipstick
£7.99 (pbk) ♦ 72pp ♦ 2007
978-1-871551-94-5

Michael CULLUP
A Change of Season
£9.95 (pbk) ♦ 98pp ♦ 2010
978-1-906075-38-5

Michael CULLUP
Matelot
£11.99 (pbk) ♦ 132pp ♦ 2016
978-1-906075-95-8

Simon DAVID
a rainbow of only one hue
£11.95 (pbk) ♦ 96pp ♦ 2016
978-1-910996-99-7

John GREENING
Hunts: Poems 1979-2009
£7.99 (pbk) ♦ 262 pp ♦ 2009
978-1-906075-33-0

Sean HALDANE
The Memory Tree
£9.99 (pbk) ♦ 90pp ♦ 2015
978-1-906075-94-1

Sean HALDANE
Always Two: Poems 1966-2009
£15.99 (pbk) ♦ 268pp ♦ 2009
978-1-906075-22-4

Ralph HODGSON
The Last Blackbird & Other Poems
£7.95 (pbk) ♦ 68pp ♦ 2004
978-1-871551-81-5

Warren HOPE
First Light & Other Poems
£9.99 (pbk) ♦ 60pp ♦ 2013
978-1-906075-80-4

Warren HOPE
Adam's Thoughts in Winter
£4.99 (pbk) ♦ 46pp ♦ 2001
978-1-871551-40-2

Gordon JARVIE
A Man Passing Through
£16.99 (pbk) ♦ 252pp ♦ 2014
978-1-906075-89-7

John LUCAS
Portable Property
£9.99 (pbk) ♦ 82pp ♦ 2015
978-1-910996-00-3

Hollie MCNISH
Papers
£11.95 (pbk) ♦ 76pp ♦ 2012
978-1-906075-67-5

Derwent MAY
Wondering About Many Women
£7.99 (pbk) ♦ 46pp ♦ 2011
978-1-906075-62-0

Robert NYE
An Almost Dancer
£7.99 (pbk) ♦ 58pp ♦ 2012
978-1-906075-39-2

Robert NYE
The Rain and the Glass
£6.99 (pbk) ♦132pp ♦ 2004
978-1-871551-41-9

Steven O'BRIEN
Scrying Stone
£7.99 (pbk) ♦ 70pp ♦ 2010
978-1-906075-56-9

Marnie POMEROY
Blue Moon
£9.99 (pbk) ♦ 76pp ♦ 2015
978-1-910996-02-7

Marnie POMEROY
The Flaming
£7.99 (pbk) ♦ 80pp ♦ 2010
978-1-906075-43-9

Martin SEYMOUR-SMITH
Collected Poems 1943-1993
£9.99 (pbk) ♦ 184pp ♦ 2006
978-1-871551-47-1

Martin SEYMOUR-SMITH
Wilderness
£4.99 (pbk) ♦ 52pp ♦ 1994
978-1-871551-08-2

David SUTTON
No Through Road
£9.99 (pbk) ♦ 48pp ♦ 2013
978-1-906075-77-4

Jim C. WILSON
Come Close and Listen
£9.99 (pbk) ♦ 88pp ♦ 2014
978-1-906075-85-9

Stephen WILSON
Fluttering Hands
£7.95 (pbk) ♦ 80pp ♦ 2008
978-1-906075-19-4

To find out more about these and other titles visit
www.greenex.co.uk